The Weight Of Wildflowers

A Collection of Poems

Ria Kaushik

BookLeaf
Publishing

India | USA | UK

Made with ❤ on the BookLeaf Publishing Platform
www.bookleafpub.in
www.bookleafpub.com

Dedication

This book is dedicated to my past self, who navigated the journey of marriage and motherhood with courage and grace, learning and evolving at every step. It is also for my future self, who, armed with these lessons, will continue to strive fearlessly towards new heights.

To the life that blossomed within me, giving me the strength and purpose to pursue my dreams—you are my greatest inspiration.

And to my partner, who stood by me unfailingly, offering his arms for comfort and his words for motivation whenever I faltered. Your unwavering support and faith have been my guiding light, keeping me steadfast on the path I set for myself.

With all my love and gratitude...

Preface

Poetry, to me, is a way of unraveling the threads of life—each verse a delicate attempt to understand the world within and around. This collection is not just a series of poems but fragments of my soul, pieced together from moments of clarity, chaos, love, and longing.

Every poem in this book was born from a genuine place—a quiet thought during a restless night, an emotion too fierce to contain, or a memory that refused to fade. Sharing these verses with you, I hope that you might find something familiar in them—a line that resonates, a metaphor that stirs, or a truth that feels like your own.

This collection is a journey, and like all journeys, it is uneven and imperfect, filled with stumbles and discoveries. Some poems are questions left unanswered, while others offer solace in their simplicity. Through them, I have tried to capture the beauty of impermanence and the weight of unsaid words.

If these poems can offer you even a moment of reflection, if they can echo something you have felt but never spoken, then I have shared them well. Thank you for holding these words, even if just for a little while.

Acknowledgements

Writing this book has been a journey of growth, reflection, and countless revisions—one that I could not have undertaken alone. I am immensely grateful to those who stood by me, encouraged me, and helped shape these poems into what they are today.

To my husband, your words of encouragement and belief in my voice have been my greatest motivation to write better with each passing day. Thank you for being my pillar of strength, for your patience during late writing nights, and for celebrating every small victory along the way.

To my friends, thank you for your invaluable feedback, thoughtful suggestions, and keen eyes for detail. Your honest critiques and encouraging words made each poem stronger. This book is a reflection of your kindness and generosity as much as it is of my own efforts.

I am truly grateful to each one of you for your support; it has been a gift I will always cherish.

With all my love and appreciation,
Ria Kaushik

1. Stepping stone
-one step towards the dream

The sun had set; through glass it spilled,
A hush of amber, soft and stilled.
It brushed my face, a fleeting glow,
Gilding spoons in molten gold.
From clay to cup, the tea uncurled,
Like restless thoughts that roamed my world.

It felt like a wish, a silent plea,
A hunger that ached so endlessly.
A touch as soft as woven lace,
Warmth spilling free in boundless streams,
A breath held still in fragile dreams,
Like amber light in glass encased.

I dreamt of you before your name,
A murmur heard, yet soft and tame.
Before your breath could brush my heart,
You lingered where the silence grew,
A thought that time already knew,

And nestled deep like morning dew.

I held you close, nested in my dreams,
A glow that shone in silver beams.
A breath so soft, a hope so true,
I traced your hands, your eyes so bright,
Felt love take shape in golden light,
A blossom waiting to ignite.

And then came waiting, hushed and slow,
The space between each heartbeat's flow.
A longing laced in silent prayers,
Would you be mine? Would you be near?
Would you call this body home, my dear?
I asked the stars, yet silence grew.

Then morning stretched, a dream untold,
A hush of knowing, soft yet bold.
Not thought, but something deep and bright,
A cradle formed where once was none,
A twitch, a spark, a rising sun,
A life now spun, two hearts as one.

The test was ink, a line so small,
Yet love had swelled beyond its call.
A quiet joy, profound and free,
Like ocean waves that kiss the shore,

A boundless depth, forevermore,
A love that time could not outgrow.

I breathed you in, the world stood still,
Each moment bent to match my will.
The sky held breath, the earth grew light,
From wish to truth, my heart had known,
Before my arms, before you'd grown,
That I was yours—you were my own.

2. Becoming
-the expansion of life

A pulse so quiet yet so true,
a whisper hidden from the eye.
No sense- no sight, no touch, no clue—
Oh! Will this time just fly by?

Two lines appear, so faint, so blue,
upon a stick of little worth.
Yet who could know if life breaks through,
which seed now stirs beneath the earth?

The fateful night when I came to know,
I tossed and turned in my bed,
awake, I dreamt- a bright ribbon, or was it a bow?
All in good stead, all in good stead.

My ribs expand, my body sways,
a temple formed in sacred light.
The aching back, the weary days—
yet love makes everything feel right.

And one day, it was bare, so rare,
a flutter deep inside my belly.
Was that you there? Oh, here then, there
Counting the kicks, keeping a tally!

Now, every day, I feel you grow,
an ounce, a stretch, a breath, that kick
My body bends, my footsteps slow;
My face looks dull or does it glow?

The nights are long, the days flee.
And then one long, endless night,
I curled in pain, my body tight.
The time had come for you to see
all that you had experienced through me.

The ticker ticked, the timings turned,
the medicines mended, the murmurs swirled.
The mother twirled, the father—
sent out a prayer into the world.

I cradle time, I breathe you in,
a world remade from what has been.
For in this space, so wild, so free,
'We' are becoming, through you, in me.

3. Dear husband -the things unsaid

The mundane routine we follow
the jobs we do, and tasks in hand
Dear husband, to you I ask
Is this where we wished to land?

We start our day with staring on screens
And so does our night ends with
Dear husband, to you I ask
Is this how we forgot to breathe?

We used to dream of working out
And now all we do is work things out
Dear husband, to you I ask
Togetherness, how did we lose this bout?

We do take care of our girls together
Their daily chores, our priority they turned
Dear husband, to you I ask
Through all of this, did our love out-burned?

I know you'd say it wasn't me or you
I know this was about what we choose
Dear husband, to you I ask
When did it become about if we win or lose?

We did the best to raise our herd
In scattered places, times; our love we sacrifice
Dear husband, to you I say
We did make our peace; does this suffice?.

Our hands grew tired, but not our bond,
Let's turn once more to love beyond.

Our love still waits, in quiet grace,
A step toward you, a warm embrace.

Through weary days and silent nights,
We'll find our way, we'll reignite.

Not lost, not gone—just left to find,
Love's not behind us, but entwined.

4. Prayers
-the ones unheard

With joint hands,
I sat to pray.
Hear me out,
Let me not fray.

I ask thee lord
Did I do wrong?
When I was hit,
Stood quiet all along.

Whose misdeed was it
When I prayed to thee
'Save me', from the flames,
they thought, it were to set me free

Who was it—deceitful,
When he lawfully wed me
But every day, demanded more
More money, more me, will he let me be?

Why was it not a felony
A crime most heinous in history
My parts wretched, what was called 'privacy'?
Tearing me, the beasts unchained, what was left as
mystery?

For how long will silence shield the crime?
How long will pain be lost in time?
Must we still beg, must we still plead,
For a world where wounds no longer bleed?

5. In you I see
-love, friendship and everything in between

In you, I see
the friend I seek,
a harbor holding steadfast still.
Through tempests, trials, tides untamed,
you anchor me with iron will.

In you, I see
the love I long for,
a flame that flickers, never fades.
Brick by brick, your boundless strength
keeps shadows soft and fears at bay.

In you, I see
a bond unbroken,
woven tight in threads of trust.
You held me high, through storms and silence,
lifting love from loss to lustrous.

In you, I see
devotion deep,
your gaze, a glow that lights my way.
Through every role, each dream I chase,
you fan the fire, you let me blaze.

In you, I see
my heart's reflection,
a soul entwined, both wild and free.
With you, I walk, with you, I wonder—
for in you, love is home to me.

6. Am I aware?
-the being

Around me there are
A thousand events taking place
In a synchronous beat
A butterfly fluttered by
And so did the bee hum its song

Am I aware?
Of what goes around me?
This question always tickles me,
The answer still to be found.

Inside me there churn
A thousand feelings rushing
In a synchronous beat
A flush of blood rushed to my face
His gaze! My tummy rumbled too!

Am I aware?
Of what goes inside me?

This question always tickles me,
The answer still to be found.

Always surrounded by people
A thousand different intentions
In a synchronous beat
One may think highly of me
The other may think- oh, poor me!

Am I aware?
Of what goes inside their heads?
This question always tickles me,
The answer still to be found.

Time moves unseen,
A thousand moments slipping
In a synchronous beat.
Yesterday's laughter fades too soon,
Tomorrow arrives before I blink.
Am I aware?
Of time's quiet thievery?
This question always tickles me,
The answer still to be found.

7. To fight for -what to live for

You wake up and see the shimmer
Glinting across your room
That one swift sweep of light—
Something worth fighting for

Sitting by his side, tea sipped slowly
Watching the flowers bloom.
Embraced by a morning kiss
Love in his eyes— worth fighting for.

Leaving home together for work,
Bidding goodbye, wishing—
To cuddle once more, wrapped in a warm hug,
Blessings, all— worth fighting for.

Touching the newborn— a kiss, a hug—
To the one, a part of you.
That first yawn, first step, her first reach
For your arms- worth fighting for.

Famished by the end, returning home,
Longing for rest, longing—
To sleep, even catch up on a short nap,
To ease the weight of the day— worth fighting for.

All day long, the small things are all,
The very essence of longing.
Not just wants, but what nurtures the soul—
These small things- all worth fighting for.

8. Stillness of the night -silence slips in

In the quiet of the night
Sitting in a quiet corner
Slipping through the tides of time
Some place- my thoughts did wander.

A shadow embarking on me
Called upon me daringly
To enter into the stillness of the night
And chase upon the dreams, warily.

I ran through my beliefs
A quick check on my opinions
On who I really wished to be, why?
Will I be the boss? Be one of the 'minions'?

A journey loud or feeble
Will it ever make the sound
The sound I wished the world to hear
Can I make an impact- oh so profound?

My callings rushed back
Woke me up from the trance
The fate written for me- sang its song
Reminded- all this was never up for a chance.

My choices were decided
'Fate', they claimed- in life
But I know I have shattered barriers,
And these thoughts of mine- just the first strife.

9. Where happiness grows -the light within

I searched for joy in fleeting hands,
In borrowed light, in shifting sand.
But every step on foreign land
Led me back to where I stand.

I chased the sun, yet clouds remained,
I sought the stars, but shadows grew.
No other soul can break my chains,
No borrowed spark can light my view.

The world will turn, the tides will sway,
The winds may steal, the skies may weep.
Yet in my heart, I hold the way—
A fire that's mine, forever deep.

No need to beg the storm to cease,
No need to chase what will not stay.
For peace was never theirs to lease,
But mine to find in my own way.

Like rivers carve the mighty stone,
Like dawn still breaks though night is long,
I shape my fate, I stand alone,
Yet in myself, I now belong.

So here I bloom, no roots unbound,
No need for hands to pull me through.
For happiness is never found—
It grows in me, it starts anew.

10. Love's Ebb and Flow

-flowing in it

Some days, love feels lost,
silent dinners, distant stares,
words too sharp to hold.

Rain falls on the glass,
you sigh, scrolling on your phone,
worlds apart, yet close.

Mornings turn to dust,
routines weighing on our hearts,
love misplaced in time.

Yet some nights, we laugh,
your hand reaches out for mine,
soft, like whispered stars.

Coffee waits for me,
you left a note on the cup—
"Drive safe, don't skip meals."

Through storms and still seas,
love is neither gone nor set,
just waves, moving on.

11. Sunshine after rain -the bonds unchanged

Haven't had a good day, workplace just isn't the same
Finding steps, tracing my way, my fingers autodial.
I look around to find my friends, ones smiling from the
frame,
One that lies upon my desk, reminded me of 'the trial'.

The jokes we shared, the dreams we spun, now echoes in
the air,
The lunch breaks filled with endless talks, now silence
fills the chair.
The clock still ticks, the tasks remain, yet something's
out of place,
Familiar walls, yet foreign now—time's left an empty
space.

The bond we built, the fights we had, the lessons that we
learned,
Like pages from a storybook, now fragile, slightly
burned.

Yet somewhere deep within my heart, their voices still
remain,
And though they're gone, their laughter hums—a
whisper in the rain.

Yet distance fails to dim the bond, even in absence—they
dissolve all pain,
A message brightens up my screen, like sunshine after
rain.
They check on me when skies are gray, they know just
what to say,
Though paths have changed, our hearts still meet in
laughter far away.

12. Twisted Sonnet

How do I love thee? Let me count the ways.

I love thee in the whisper of the storms,
I love thee under silver moonlit skies,
I love thee as the autumn leaves transform,
I love thee where the spring's first petals rise.

I love thee through the hush of falling snow,
I love thee while the mighty sun ascends,
I love thee in the moments lost and slow,
Where time dissolves, yet love transcends.

But can mere words thy depth express?
Wilt thou be ever truly mine?
Come closer, love, and softly press—
For thee art evermore as thine.

And though the stars may fade and shadows flee,
My love shall live, unbound, eternally.

13. The Search

His glinting eyes—oh! How brown they were!
Piercing through my soul, seeking the unknown.
Trusting the gut, searching everywhere,
Yet I sat right through it—still and alone.

Sparkling with tears, squinting to stop the drop,
Trickling down his face—the pain that had grown.
Fearfully still, his gaze held the teary lop,
Yet I sat right through it—ever so still and glum.

Squinching his eyes shut, he prayed I would say,
Yearning for words to prove he wasn't forlorn.
Love still undying, yet fading away,
Yet I sat right through it—ever so still and glum.

Agonizing, his eyes gave one last painful glare,
Reaching for his face, I let out a final moan.
His search had ended as my soul lay bare,
Truce made with truth, the words softly shone:

*"Darling, my love for you is a constant—perish never be.
Your search is over—right through my eyes, you see."*

14. Unmatched

I have to tell you a tale,
A tale of a wise, strong man,
Blessed with judgment, firm and sure,
A heart that knew, a hand that steered,
To set things right—yes, he can.

But as nature always wills,
Where a path is true and bright,
Lurks another, shadowed deep,
And so there came into his life
A love that stole his sight.

She called herself his dearest,
And love, she did proclaim.
She took his heart within her grasp,
Yet left him with his rightful share—
A love that burned, yet pained.

And all this time, he knew it well,
Her love had made him blind.

Yet still, he walked, though steps unsteady,
Bound to share a life with her—
A life where blame entwined.

"Did she never love him?"
His daughter had to know.
He closed his eyes and softly spoke,
"There was no love so beautiful
As the one she once let go."

Yet even knowing all the scars,
He could not love her less.
For hidden deep within her cries,
Was love unspoken, love suppressed.

She lived entranced within a storm,
A love that bruised her soul.
Yet through the years, she saw the truth—
His heart, though strong as wood,
Was carved with edges fine and whole.

"Can he love her once again?"
A thought she could not break.
Yet the father smiled and whispered low,
"Her fight has just begun, my child—
His love is hers to take."

The warmth of love he gave to her
Had taught her all along.
Her hands now held the strength she needed
To pen the final lines—
To finish their love song.

She braved the climb, she bore the storm,
Her every instinct matched.
And there she stood when he would fall,
Arms open, steady, strong,
To catch him in her grasp.

He knew his fall would drain him pale,
Leave him weak upon his bed.
But there she stood with bloodshot eyes,
With love to pour, with care to give,
And tears for love—unmatched.

The wood-hard heart grew soft once more
At the whisper of her touch.
As flowers bloomed, love stretched its arms,
No longer pain, no longer curse—
Just love returned as much.

"It's all too poetic, no truth to tell,"
His mother softly wept.
"The man was pure, a soul divine,

And she—she shone again in love,
No dark clouds left behind."

And there she stood, a guardian firm,
As he lay upon his bed.
Yet still within her eyes he saw,
Love to pour, care to give,
And tears for love—unmatched.

15. Iridescence

Lit up orange, the ground did burn,
Yet I lifted myself to walk upon it.
Tingling my skin, sunlight I yearned,
Each ember flared, my spirit lit.

Glistening waters—so was my soul,
As I gazed into its endless deep.
Reflections danced, yet none were whole,
Merging with moss in currents steep.

I turned green, then blue, then gold,
Iridescence wrapped me tight.
My cries, unheard, grew faint and cold,
Breaking free from worldly ties.

With will and ink, the hues took shape,
Etched upon me, raw and bright.
A heartbeat marked—a fleeting scrape,
A stain of color, pure delight.

Yet time dissolves all marks we bear,
Each hue, each wound, each fleeting chain.
Fading softly into air,
As does the ink, so does the pain.

16. So Done!

I lived by a motto, one that said,
"Keep pushing forward, stay ahead."
Through storms and trials, pain and fight,
I held my ground, I chased the light.

I bit my tongue, I played it fair,
I carried burdens, grinned, and bore,
I gave my best, beyond my share,
Yet they still wanted more.

I was the rock, the one who stayed,
The one who healed, the one who prayed.
I held the weight, I stood my ground,
But where was love when I broke down?

So done with bending, done with pain,
Done with walking through the rain.
If kindness means to bleed and burn,
Then maybe it's my turn to learn.

No more waiting, no more chains,
No more playing losing games.
I lived by a motto, but now I see—
It's time to start living just for me.

17. Elation

Her joy spread
Spread like a wing
Across her face I knew in a blink
It was her smile
Stretching
Miles, across the vast expanse.

I danced
Jumped and sang
Day and night
The sound rang, a melody bright and clear
It was her elation
Unbound
Happiness, it spread.

18. The Weight of the Wildflowers

I continued walking but slouched—
Not by the weight of objects I carried,
Moving things and organizing my place,
But by the burden of responsibilities
Under the load that I was buried.

Being part of any relationship,
One expects to share the load—
Which otherwise is carried by one.
Some days I find that there is none;
I am to blame, hold up, stay in work mode.

That fire in me, some days, does burn—
The same one that had once burned out.
It lights me up with my desire to give,
Not to expect what I'd get in return.
In the end, giving my love is all this is about.

I continue walking, no longer slouched—

The love in me helping me carry it all for hours,
Building my place, livening things around,
Only with that hand reaching out to me,
Reminding me of the weight of my wildflowers.

19. Break free

The leaf, stuck to the branch,
Hung by a short string of cells,
Still craved and desired for a—
Longing, longing for a dance.

A dance to show its poise,
Unshaken by how you may see.
The swirls and waves it created,
Yearning for one call from that voice.

A voice that swooshes through,
That shatters branches, old and new.
The wind, relentless as it blew—
The leaf broke free and finally flew.

20. Addict

Four-thirty chimed on the clickety clock,
Splashed and rubbed my eyes, craving sleep.
Caught in a glance what glared from the mirror—
A hollow expression, cold and mock.

My own face stared back with no remorse;
It spoke, in one shot, all it could:
The guilt, the pain, the pity—a love failed,
My addiction to him was my own curse.

Hundreds of hours, days, months, and years—
None would matter, I knew, as they passed.
I loved him purely; his leaving me behind
Will forever inflict pain and drop tears.

The last he spoke, he promised eternity,
He swore he'd love me till his last breath.
He kept his promise—couldn't cheat death.
I was to die then—only he found serendipity.

21. Grave Truth

From blood's red with blacks and whites,
Merging in water's salty turquoise,
Erasing stained proofs, see how lights
Balance the shades, brimmed with poise.

Now it wears blue of stress, shimmering,
Miming its way to others' green.
Over and over, both glittering,
Whispering gloom in fluttering sheen.

In the end, you lie for all colors murdered—
They came, curdled, seeking a way out.
I stood there alone, body shuddered,
Lost for words, without a scout.

The day is done, yet no one listened—
My griefs cried loud, unseen, unsought.
Colors faded, only gray glistened,
And now on my grave, they bow and fault.